WALLOON WRITERS REVIEW

FOURTH EDITION

Walloon Writers Review is an independent literary magazine sharing amateur and professional creative writing and photography inspired by the natural beauty of the northern Michigan region. A portion of all submissions fees for the Fourth Edition will be donated to Walloon Lake Trust and Conservancy and Tip of the Mitt Watershed Council, non profit corporations that are committed to preservation of the natural resources of the region.

Walloon Writers Review accepts submissions of original creative writing and photography with a specific focus of Northern Michigan and Michigan's Upper Peninsula. For information, visit www.walloonwriters.com.

Walloon Writers Review
P.O. Box 2460
Petoskey, Michigan 49770
www.walloonwriters.com

Editor: Jennifer Huder
Cover photo: Rumblings on the Little Bay by Kelly Tingle Kazmierski
Produced by MissionPointPress.com

Walloon Writers Review (ISSN 2572-9683)

ISBN: 978-1-943995-90-5
Library of Congress Control Number: 2018960576

CONTENTS

Crooked Tree Arts Center & Petoskey News Review
16th Annual Young Writers Juried Exposition
Winning Poetry and Prose
from Elementary, Middle and High School

THOMAS CONLAN

North Woods Dream

A walk in white woods, no ruffed grouse. A few deer trails. On the ground, paw depressions, pad marks molded, wolf tracks.

An owl sweeps low, fills the sky. Wings span the width of the path beneath tunneled trees.

The sun sets through white branches overhanging the Escanaba River.

A familiar face shines briefly within a yellow moon, now hidden by winsome clouds.

A wolf howls. The moon a wanting mistress, leaves, reveals a fleeting glimpse, only to leave again.

I demur, safe in cabin walls where gas lights flicker. A pretzel with my bourbon and ice. Snow melts by the wood stove.
Salt absorbs and swirls in brown liquid.

Oh my, her gentle voice.

He pounds to the heavens, haunted, questions never answered.

The answer lies within, says the moon glowing in quiet meditation.

No, without, I cry aloud to the sky, to the moon and planets and stars, to the universe.

No one hears. Alone in the north woods. And in the evening before a woodstove snow melts slowly.

Again the moons shows herself, her reverential light.

Oh my, she says, snow.

View of The Beast by Kelly Tingle Kazmierski

GLEN YOUNG

Ava Gardner, Casting for Native Brook Trout, Somewhere along the Yellow Dog River, 1954

Ava Gardner was here, in the stream, fly rod
in hand, knee deep in these mechanics of mystery,
fairytale and instructional manual,
calling out "ten and two, ten and two,"
while I worked my knots, the line
slippery with reverie in the dark pool,
a heron slowly beating the air overhead.
"Ten and two" she called again,
her slender vernal fingers,
those woodsy sunlit eyes,
that minor waterfall of auburn curls,
the cedars and the riffles—all of these
and more—bathed in river light.

GLEN YOUNG

Men Grooming Horses

Men grooming horses at eventide
in shaded barns atop our hill,
flies quiet, the breeze calmed,
and you, contented at the table,
the sweep of your back and shoulders—
the jewel of your neck—
proof enough how the earth is round,
as each black night gives way
again to a next dawn, evidence
god remembers us still.

Miss Millay and Me

Whether New England or these Great Lakes,
we'd note a fence, some over-large greenery,
perhaps a dog or two, birds lighting in the quaking limbs
ahead of dusk, our voices in song or silent in pause,
in wonder at some clouds overhead.
Miss Millay and me, my Edna at the fence, clear-headed
and curious in the loam of our commingled verse.

Bridge Wash by Linda Gall

PHILLIP STERLING

The First Morning

Fog rises before me
solitary, east in every window

beyond which the field—
lazy with summer's ancient grass—

falls back into slumber
its greeting not ready to be sound

On the table a simple breakfast:
coffee, a piece of fruit, a nod

to the presence of day's imprecision
time having nothing to do with it

I linger, let grasshoppers' wings
dry   before I begin

PHILLIP STERLING

Another Day

The sun admires its reflection
in the east window of the vacant farmhouse

thinking it has no competition
despite the attention of the boy walking past

who knows better   having picked
from the last tree of the old orchard

standing beside the road named for the people
of the farm   a thousand apples

each with the radiance of morning

Evening Glory by Kelly Tingle Kazmierski

GREG RAPPLEYE

Missing Woman Found Alive in Quarry

— *The Straitsland Resorter, June 25, 1973*

She was going to mass at St. Monica's
with a fifth of Knob Creek and a go-cup of ice
scoured from the sputtery ice machine,
when darkness took her—often, these takings—
who knew where she might run? We saw her
bottom out the blue Town Car, whirr gravel
at the restaurant drive, then turn the county road
toward Afton—lofting over the Michigan Central,
up the Sandy, and past the rickety fire tower.
For hours, that's all we knew. Beyond the icy
Pigeon River, mother turned left instead of right—
she *must* have—wheeled north, then swerved
down a two-track, through brackens and jack pines.
She missed an arrow sprayed on plywood
and launched from the cut of the limestone quarry,
went airborne some thirty feet out, out over
the green water—so far out, my brother proposed
a Family Puzzler: How fast was mother traveling
when the drive wheels of her two-and-a-half ton Lincoln
lost touch with the quarry rim? With proofs to be
written as limericks, wax-sealed in manila fold-ups
for however long it took, and read at mother's wake.
Who dreamed she would live another forty-five years?
It was a dust year, the summer of grass fires,
the quarry pond was low and the Town Car sank
only to its adjustable mirrors; no deeper.
Before sunset we found her—silent, unhurt,
seated atop the vinyl roof, among the water lilies
and damsel flies, the bluegills and punkies stippling
the quiet pond. She stared at the fractured walls
and gravel shoals of the quarry, like a cursed woman
in some Pre-Raphaelite canvas, leaning into the day's
last light; almost, it seemed, poised to weep a desperate
question from the thwarts of her sturdy blue boat,
or an another might have once believed,
almost ready, *bel canto*, to sing.

Pictured Rocks Shore by Katrina Valuyeva

BRETT ALLEN

Pine River Raid

They'd sent in their first scout just after dusk, when the day's last light flickered out over a carpet of white oak tree-tops. It's hard to say how long he'd been watching us. Four of us there on the ridge, huddled around summer flames, periodically shifting camp-chairs or reciting wives'-tale chants in defense of wandering smoke.

"I hate dead rabbits. I hate dead rabbits. I hate dead rabbits."

I don't know where his boldness came from. Perhaps his friends were rabbits. Or perhaps he figured we were too engaged in our fireside philosophizing to notice, but a careless step and a broken twig were all it took to put him center stage in four converging flashlight beams. He stared at us a moment. And we, at him. Him, sizing us up or perhaps failing to realize how caught he really was. Us, scouring our raccoon-knowledge-data-banks and hoping someone else would make the first move.

Adam stomped his foot and the bandit crashed off into the thick curtain of bracken ferns. Thank God we'd brought an Eagle Scout.

We turned back to the fire with nervous chuckles and bold talk, but our ears were elsewhere. The fire crackled, sending tiny embers dancing overhead before disappearing among the fireflies that dotted the steep ravine to the Pine River's waters far below.

Soon the encounter was all but forgotten, our vigilance replaced with yawns and stretches.

We tidied the area, packing half-empty bags of chips and cheap hot dogs into rubber totes and coolers. An open can of baked beans was left on the far side of the fire. A sacrifice to appease the forest varmints. All other food was out-of-sight-out-of-mind and we retreated to our respective tents.

Sleep was evasive, between the hard ground and baying coyotes who were much too close for comfort. Before long, the call-of-the-wild trailed off into the deep woods, replaced only by the rustling oak leaves above and the occasional, startling drone of a mosquito grazing my ear. A light snore rumbled from the tent next to me and a previously unnoticed root pushed through my thin sleeping mat, providing unsolicited lumbar support. My eyes finally closed.

"RRRRRRRT"

My eyes open. The unmistakable sound of tiny claws against textured plastic. An empty beer can clatters to the ground. The snoring in the neighboring tent stops. From the campsite, a spat amongst thieves. The invaders hiss like cougars and bark like rottweilers. For a moment, it seems all forest-creation has descended on our campsite to lay claim to bruised bananas and white bread burger buns. Through the thin canvas, the shriek of a tent zipper. Adam is on the move. I can't let a friend die alone, so I grab my flashlight and join him on the path back to the fire pit. Our comrades are still sleeping, pretending not to hear it, or perhaps dead already.

Adam moves like a ninja. I, like a drunken lumberjack. The coals in the fire pit still glow like a porthole to hell and we stop our advance at the black edge of the moonlit clearing. On the fold-out camp table, one of the bandits rests on his haunches, his head consumed by a peanut butter jar. Beside the table, a cooler sits open with its lid facing toward us. We can hear the second scavenger rattling within. Adam silently counts down on his fingers.

3-2-1

We click our lights simultaneously, illuminating the debauchery of these Pine River plunderers. Adam charges, his howl mimicking the coyotes. I follow suit. My howl is more beagle than beast. To our delight, the first raccoon's head had, in fact, become lodged inside the peanut butter jar. His desperation is palpable. In his panic, he backpedals too far and crashes hard to the ground below. With all four paws, he pries the jar from his butter-lathered face and thunders blindly into the bushes, joining his comrade who, just as quickly, has vacated the open cooler.

Adam and I stand silent, listening to the ferns breaking farther and farther away. A glint flashes off the blade in Adam's hand.

"You had a knife this whole time?" I asked.

"Well, duh," he says. "That could've been a black bear for all I knew."

I let that sink in, as Adam surveys the damage and begins securing the area again. Our battle cries were enough to wake our compatriots whom now stumble around the site, muttering questions through their yawns. Adam does his best to answer their concerns or at least the ones he can understand.

"Yes, they were raccoons."

"Yes, they were big."

"Yes, they'll be back."

"Yes, they eat people."

The raided cooler has no latch, so we stack a smaller cooler on top. Adam hands me his knife and I cut strips of duct tape as he adds one last layer of security. With everything sealed again, we march off, single file, down the trail back to our tents, confident that we're now prepared. We are halfway back before I realize I've left Adam's knife on the table. I double back to retrieve our meager bear defense, but freeze after only a few steps.

In the middle of the trail, silhouetted by the glow of distant coals, stands a raccoon the size of a wolf. Or so it seems. He stares at me down the barrel of my flashlight, a scar dividing a cloudy eye on his right side. His lip quivers, unleashing a sound akin to grinding gravel. A charge and a howl will not unseat *this* forest gladiator.

Searching the ground around me, my eyes land on a stick of considerable girth. I bend over, keeping the spotlight trained on the prehistoric rodent. The stick feels like a relayer's baton, but of solid oak. Before my brain can reason with my arm, I've heaved a mighty throw at the brigand before me. The baton flies true, striking the beast across the torso with a hollow thud.

The raccoon is unmoved. Unnerved. Unimpressed.

It looks down at the stick with contempt. Then back to me, as the embers in its eyes churn into an inferno. Leaning forward, it bawls like some other-worldly hellcat. It charges.

"Run!" I scream, slamming down the trail after my friends. They require no further instruction.

One, two, three, four, we plow into a single tent, Adam slashing the zipper shut behind us. Silence. We wait for razor claws to shred the canvas walls, but they never come. We listen intently for minutes that feel like hours.

Enough time passes for us to think we're in the clear.

And that's when it starts again. Claws on textured plastic. Cans rattling. A volley of wild threats. We look to Adam.

"Everything is locked down," he whispers. "They won't be able to get at any food tonight. Once they realize that, they'll leave."

A new noise joins the fray. A long, dragging noise, repeating rhythmically in comparison to the chaos around.

"It sounds like they're dragging a body," I whisper.

I do a quick count to make sure we are all present.

"What is--"

I'm silenced as Adam raises a finger into the air. He's at full alert and tilts his head like a cocker spaniel. His eyes go wide.

"They're pushing the cooler away," he exclaims, jerking the zipper open again.

He charges out. We follow with borrowed courage and an overwhelming desire not be left alone in the tent.

We are halfway to the clearing when the real tragedy strikes. There is a loud crash, followed by another, and another. The destruction plunges down the ravine. They were not pushing the cooler away after all. They were pushing it over the edge. We reach the clearing just in time to hear the final bounce and the icy splash of the cooler hitting the river, two hundred feet below. The raccoons have gone. Our approach had not been stealthy.

We shine our lights over the steep bank. Food litters the hill, snagged by sandbars, ferns, and sapling white pines. A loaf of bread has exploded, leaving a patchwork of white lily pads, reflecting moonlight. An emptied egg carton hangs from a tree branch, while a punctured soda-can hisses its dying breath beneath it.

An attempt is made to recover the cooler and we collect food wrappers and cooking utensils as we descend to the river below. All is for naught. The cooler has become a sacrifice to the river-gods. It is never seen again. Like Hansel and Gretel, the bread trail is gone when we make our ascent back to camp. Defeated, the others return to their tents. Before I follow, I check the open can of beans. It is untouched. From down the hill, a twig snaps. Coyotes bay in the distance.

Grand Traverse Bay Morning Moon by Charles Rammelkamp

JESSE LINCOLN

North

Go

Find something

Away from the city

In some far-off hills

Along clear, fast rivers

Under star-drenched nights

Bathe in the silver gospel of the moon

Run into the big lake

So that it may wash over your heart

So that it may beat to the cadence of the waves

Get lost under the oldest trees

Give your mind to their wilds

Hear sky sing to pine

That pure wind unfolding

Weaving melody through swaying limbs

A summer song played on wind-bent tree

The sacred anthem of the north

UP Falls by Steven W. Huder

SHARON RUFF

Holy Land

Every fall, when my feet kiss the earth
on our 80 acres in Northern Michigan, I become whole.
My lungs expand, sucking in more woodsy air
than they can possibly hold.
My eyes awaken. I twirl around and
hug the glory of fields, steams, valleys and ponds.

The spinning leaves of the poplars
wave "Hello! We've missed you,"
and the majestic oaks nod their greeting like
silent sentries guarding the land.
I pause often,
overcome by the sacredness of the moment.

The barren mound by the sandpit awaits
my ritual assent where I fling my arms out wide
and shout, YES, YES, YES never knowing where that yes will lead.
The wind of spirit blows through me
purging the lint of life from every pore.
For a flicker of time I am permeable and at one with this land.

MELISSA SEITZ

Depth of Field

Murmurous voices float across the frozen lake,
confusing my solitude, echoing my ineptitude.
My camera becomes my eyes in the dark.
Momentarily exposed, I am Selene
in flashes of silver and white.

The lullaby of a great horned owl
filters through the cold night air.
The wolf moon slides up
a pulsing vein of darkened sky.
My camera captures its journey.

I imagine you watching me
as you once did, my camera
capturing the space between us.

If only I had understood the photographs:
You were always looking elsewhere
under my constant watch.

Sunrise with Morning Moon by Melissa Seitz

MILTON BATES

Naturalized

Approaching our feeder for the first time,
the gray squirrel was wary, ready
to retreat if challenged. Until then

the place belonged to birds and red squirrels.
What was a gray doing among our balsams,
pines, and spruces, far from the nut trees

it favored? We assumed it was just
passing through, a youngster perhaps, off
to see the world before it settled down.

Then it reappeared with another gray.
The pair made their nest, not in the hollow
of a hardwood or hammocked on an oak branch,

but high in the crown of a white pine.
They share the Jacob's ladder of its trunk
with nuthatches and brown creepers. The reds,

though still standoffish, observe the truce
declared each winter around the feeder.
Our neighbors are as surprised as we are,

hearing about the grays. *Any sign*
there'll be a litter of little ones this spring?
they ask when we meet them on the road.

That's the kind of people they are, happy
to indulge our minor discoveries.
More momentous was the one we made

many years ago, first passing through,
when we realized our question wasn't really
a question: *What if we chose to live here?*

J.W. JORDAN

Drilling For Bats

It was an odd assortment of tools. It was an odd sort of a project. Fitting, I suppose. In hand, as I pulled the cord on the rickety spring-loaded pull-down stair set that leads up into the attic were a hand operated wood auger with a quarter inch wood boring bit, a length of old quarter inch clear plastic tubing, a small cheap cigar, a lighter and a tape measure. Well, I have a pretty good eye for distance so it was decided to leave the tape measure alone all by itself on the kitchen table. I'd regret that cockiness later. Up the stairway I went with purpose and confidence, still in my damp swimsuit and somewhat sandy crocs. It was a warm late July afternoon at Cedar Haven. There was just enough time to take care of this seemingly simple project, and who knows, it just might work.

It's amazing what can be scrounged up in the old shed off the back porch of the cottage. There are old dock spikes that have been used and reused many summers over. Not one of them remains straight. Each with at least one bend or twist from an over-zealous or errant hammer swing in the spring or the final thrust of a prying crowbar in the fall. Most are a bit rusty, some very, even the galvanized ones. All of them have been reformed and straightened, available for use on the dock again. There is also a plethora of bolts, washers and wood screws. Wood screws with hooks, wood screws with closed eye ends, wood screws with Phillips-heads, wood screws with straight-slotted heads, wood lag screws ... lots of screws used to securely connect large wooden dock parts. In a prominent, easily accessed location is a magnet tied to a string. It has been designed specifically to retrieve these old rusty spikes and screws when they roll along just out of a jutting-arms reach and then mercilessly hop off the dock's edge, plop into the water and quickly take their station on the sandy bottom below.

Along with the faded life preservers, canoe paddles, fishing poles and boat cushions one can find almost anything to successfully complete any small project around Cedar Haven if one uses the imagination. Folks with cottages along Wilderness Bay really need to be resourceful when doing a spur of the moment project.

The mainland and any supplier of hardware or equipment are a boat ride, a car ride, another car ride, and then one more boat ride away. If it's a rough day on the bay, that can take up practically a whole afternoon in itself. Substantial projects demand serious logistical planning. Even when preparation and planning has been done well, snags can really throw a monkey wrench into the works. On one occasion, I recall the successful completion of the installation of a new commode in the Cedar Haven bathroom was nearly achieved except for the final tightening of the bolts to the floor. Either it was the unevenness of the old cottage floor, or one too many turns of the wrench, but that poor toilet base cracked clean through and that was that. Last I saw, it had been heaved out the back door and was laying fractured and uncomfortable a ways up the path to the outhouse. The brand-new shine of pure white porcelain and its stylish smooth curves contrasted brilliantly with the wilds of the greens and browns of cedar boughs and birch leaves of the northern Michigan island woods.

The tossing of the cracked commode was gracefully completed and accompanied by colorful, elegant words that my young ears at the time assumed were naturally an integral part of the ceremony with yet another excursion to the mainland about to ensue. Other supply-acquiring journeys to the mainland of note over the years include a cumbersome load of twelve-foot boards to be used to reinforce attic rafters to more aptly handle the winter snow load. All were transported from the lumberyard in Cedarville to the awaiting boat in Hessel in a 1986 Buick Regal, protruding dangerously high and forward through the car's sunroof. Thankfully, there were only a few stoplights that needed to be navigated around. A few years prior, a brand-new refrigerator for my Great Aunt Gertrude was delivered on a rough Wilderness Bay day in a boat much too small for its cargo. The fridge and all souls on board, including Great Aunt Gertrude, made it safely but needless to say it was a boat ride that all involved remember to this day.

There would be no need for a trip to the mainland for this project. Today's odd assortment of equipment was found in that dependable shed, all except for the cigar. It was found merely by happenstance in the under-the-dash compartment of the Boston Whaler we were renting. I probably should have reported its usage to the renter. I'm sure there was nowhere in the fine print of the boat rental agreement anything that had to do with making available one small cheap cigar. He seems to be an understanding guy, so I hope he won't mind.

Cigar smoke is not an uncommon thing around Cedar Haven. Why, some of the finest and grandest of cigars have been clipped, lit and puffed in and around the nearby cottages. The owner of the cottage next door was the proprietor of a fine cigar and tobacco shop in Colorado which supplied the cigars of shakers and movers back in the day. The late United States Senator Ted Kennedy and even former United States Presidential candidate Walter F. Mondale were among those who enjoyed his fine tobacco cigars. Back when he smoked them, my dad was able to enjoy the same expensive and extravagant cigars that the powerful and influential enjoyed. The cigar in my hand as I made my way up the springy stairway into the attic this day is not one of them.

Bats have been cohabitating with us humans here around Cedar Haven since its beginning. Usually they can be found nervously clinging behind a window blind during the day or occasionally can be seen gracefully swooping and swerving through a summer sunset sky, skewering skeeters as they go. Encounters such as these are enjoyable and memorable. Occasionally, however, bats have been able to find their way into the cottage, usually in the middle of the night at the most inopportune time. They seem to like the cottage chimney and fireplace. Evidence of their intrusions has been found along the side of the brick fireplace where it meets the wood paneling of the living room. These access ports are immediately plugged with putty and wood filler, successfully halting any further invasions.

The squeaks and minute vibrations of a colony of bats presumably within the wall above the fireplace have been evident now for several days. It was hoped that the arrival of the noisy humans for this week of vacation would cause this band of flying bandits to go elsewhere. Such has not been the case. After some preliminary investigation, it is determined that the bat colony has taken up residence in the wall between the chimney above the fireplace and the living room with most of the activity seemingly to be further up that wall into the attic. Without knowing any better, it seems like there are many more than one, but probably not an ungodly amount. Further reconnaissance confirmed that the attic wall with the chimney on the other side is ground zero.

The attic is shadowy and darkened even on this late sunny afternoon, lit only by windows at either end of its elongated, gabled roof space. The sunny summer afternoon is unable to completely pierce the surrounding pines and birches outside so the amount of light those windows are allowing is less than helpful. That's not a big problem, though. The attic has been traversed so many times that its low rafters only caused one substantial bump of the head, causing a momentary dazed pause as I made my way toward the hanging bulb light and its dangling chain switch. Dang! Another low rafter and a somewhat longer pause this time to gather myself and rub what are now two sore spots on my forehead. Why can't I remember to bend ... even just a little? After a shake of the head, I press on. With a yank and a grinding click there is glorious light, illuminating the entire expanse of the cluttered attic, all except for a certain corner, the corner with the wall behind which the bats reside.

After manhandling an extremely heavy cast iron sink on the floor out of the way, the only things between me and the wall the bats are behind are some old hanging raincoats and an umbrella that looks to be a relic straight from the roaring twenties. Most of the raincoats are likely from the same era and probably would do little good in a light mist. One of the raincoats, though, is bright and yellow from a more modern era. On it, peculiarly written with a fat black permanent ink marker in careful printed handwriting are the words "NOT A RAINCOAT". As I studied it I began to hope that determination wasn't made during a sudden squall out on the bay halfway to Hessel. The twittering vibrations and squeaks of a colony of bats within the wall next to me brought me swiftly back to the job at hand. The heat that had built up in the attic that afternoon and multiple rafter knocks on the noggin seemed to be causing me to be a little slow.

My first objective was to determine exactly where to drill my hole. That should be easy. "Exactly" might not be the best term, though. Looking out the window I visually measured the distance from the window to the chimney. Easily, one would assume, the smack-dab center of the chimney would be less than a foot beyond that point. Wanting to be sure, though, I measured more accurately using an old, long bamboo fishing pole. So, inside now on that wall I measured that same bamboo fishing pole distance toward where the chimney would begin and added another foot. That would be my drill point. Pressing my ear to the warm, unfinished tongue and groove cedarwood wall at that spot revealed plenty of bat racket on the other side. This was it. That is the spot.

Confirmed by the latest bamboo fishing pole measuring technology. I looked and listened to be sure once more. Was I really about to drill a hole in the side of a perfectly good cottage? Really? I was confident and commenced drilling. The dry wood drilled easily once the main wood boring flutes started peeling away the cedarwood and in no time I had pushed through, thinking those poor, unsuspecting, upside-down hanging dingbats were probably wondering what the heck had just burst into their hangout. After a few awkward yanks, the drill was pulled out with a triumphant "Hah!"

Just as quickly as my achievement was assumed, confusion set in. A quarter inch shaft of sunlight immediately shot into the darkness of the attic with the simultaneous removal of the auger bit. It illuminated particulates and bits of sawdust suspended in the air like snowflakes in a headlight beam during a lake effect snow squall on a wintery night. Yeah, looks like the tape measure might have been a good idea after all. Okay, that's a bit of a setback but nothing that can't be overcome. I'll simply visually measure over the distance that would be needed to safely accommodate the width of the chimney. A new spot was identified. Once again, this was it. That was the spot. But this time I didn't even need to recheck or listen. This had to be the place. Just like the first attempt the drilling went well. Just like the first time, after a few awkward pulls the drill bit came out with a flip of small curled wood chips and dust and, ... just like the first try another quarter inch shaft of sunlight burst forth. Dang! I had now, indeed, succeeded in putting TWO holes into the side of a perfectly good cottage! Not to be dissuaded, I immediately identified the precise center point (in my best estimation without the use of the latest bamboo fishing pole measuring capabilities) between those holes and began drilling with abandon, knowing for sure I'd hit pay dirt on this attempt. Nothing but net! Straight through the uprights! Nothing could stop me now! For sure, after breaking through initially, the bit came up against the hard, scratchy surface of the cinder block chimney. No light shone through this time and those bats had to be freaking out!

Now with the successful incursion of the bat lair came the iffy part. The clear plastic tubing was inserted. A perfect fit it was, nice and snug. Next was to light that "fine" tobacco cigar and commence to puffing. The first draw produced a healthy mouthful of cigar smoke (as if there is such a thing) that was quickly blown into the tube. The grey ghostly haze zipped straight into the bat den. Piece of cake, nothing to it! After about ten puffs and blows, the fake sweetness of the cheap cigar's wooden tip became rather disagreeable and the cigar itself became hot and somewhat soggy. After another five or six puff and blows, things began to get a little woozy. The warm attic, several blows to the head and cheap cigar fumes began to cast doubt on the outcome of this supposed simple project. Finally, after about twenty puff and blows and the resultant nausea, sweatiness and head-spins, I was relieved and overjoyed to hear a ruckus from the other side of the wall. The mild squeaks and twittering vibrations from the earlier everyday bat conversations within the colony had grown now to angry shrieks and a full-blown bat uproar.

From the front deck of the cottage outside down below, I heard counting. "...Seventeen ... eighteen ... nineteen... twenty! Twenty bats have flown out! Twenty-one!" It was looking as though the colony of small nocturnal flying mammals had exited the crevice they once called home. My ear, pressed against the warm cedarwood wall hopefully one last time, confirmed the golden silence of an empty bat hideout.

This belfry was now bat-less.

Holding onto that wall, I almost passed out. I so wanted to just slouch down to the attic floor in hopes of alleviating the spins and woozy-ness but then realized I had several quarter inch holes in a perfectly good cottage wall to fill.

A simple project, really, completed easily with three small sections of quarter inch doll rod conveniently found in that old shed off the back porch.

Les Cheneaux Family Photo, J.W. Jordan

CJ GIROUX

Cloudburst

Dusk races across Lake Michigan to the marina. Its green beacon beckons over the breakwall like a firefly caught in a blue Mason jar. Stones somersault in surf; motor oil spots the shoreline; rainbows hover around each stain, shimmering like the Northern lights. We scramble toward our red-roofed cabin where the exposed corners of shingles creep upward, form black-rimmed cups, overflow. The house bleeds rain, rivulets, gullies. We remain surrounded.

ROBERT VIVIAN

August Elegy

Late summer crickets and the smell of ashes, and I still don't know where words come from, I who am leaning wildly into sound with my whole body, into the northward direction of all yearning, I still don't know where words come but holy is this foremost bent, holy and mysterious and the burnt embers from last night's fire as I listened to the birds for the songs that wake up the deep heaven within so heaven is a birdsong, heaven, my love, is right here at the delicate angle of your elbow and the lilacs long past blooming, what fey, tender grief bears such an emphasis Hamlet asked, the brave, bright yearning of a candle flame leading me to words like these even though I do not know where they come from, love, or sometimes even what they mean or that they can only mean this love and this yearning and feeling of loss, oh, elegy in the shining roundness of a teaspoon and words like these trying to find a rhythm and a cadence to sing of this loss called All My Surging Blood, oh, the rife beauty I have known, cedar trees and sweepers in the current, lilacs again and a blizzard of butterflies attending them like summer snowfall, every river which is a vein of north whose heart I dream as a great wound flowering into petal, into rosebud and maybe words like these that grow as the trees grow and by way of the same living force so tree is a poem and poem is a human mouth playing with words on his tongue, tasting them in sweetness and sometimes bitterness, honey and vinegar and Jesus refusing both on the cross because he was bleeding skyward and every dictionary be praised, my deep sweet home rhythm for words which are but symbols and playthings of love, of come late summer melancholy slowly turning into sunlight again the smell of Tina's hair fresh after the shower, stay young forever seasons of the earth as Milosz once wrote, I still don't know where words come from or what they mean or where they are going or to whom, only that I will follow them faithfully and wildly wherever they take me the rest of my days as the crickets sound their one sustained note and I just another blue-eyed witness to the truth of stamen and stone and the fish that haunts my dreams showing me the beauty of all there is or will ever be in brief rising boil of forever.

Milkweed by Melissa Seitz

CAROL OBERG

Peripheral Vision

She walks down the road
Passing trees, wildflowers, shrubs
She couldn't name in a million years.
Strolls the seasons
Without seeing the first buds,
Some oak leaves refusing to ever fall
The slow melt of ice and snow.
She doesn't notice the crickets temperate pace
Or the v's of traveling geese overhead.
If like sleeping beauty she were to
Suddenly awake with the kiss of a prince
It would be impossible to guess if it was
Late in the fall or very early spring.
She doesn't garden but buys
Flowers and produce at Farmer's Market
And appreciates a gorgeous sunset
Without the need to describe it in words
Or fix it in the lens of a camera.
Her house inside is unadorned
The yard simply grass that
Changes from green to brown
When she isn't looking

Much like herself.

But driving down a country road

When the leaves on trees are

Red, orange, yellow and every

Unnamable color in between

She thinks Heaven

Must look exactly like this.

— *first published in 'The Avocet' fall 2016*

Grand Traverse Bay Sunset by Charles Rammelkamp

CAROL OBERG

Slow goodbye

Out the upstairs window
I blow smoke
That joins company
With the smoke flying out
Of the wood furnace.
A glob of snow sits on
The brown grass
In the shape of
Michigan's Upper Peninsula.
It is the only white visible.
Likely the only bit anywhere
Not melted on this
Third day
Of May.

After the Snowfall by Steven W. Huder

ANDREA DEJEAN

Secret migration, silent

Fall

The opposite shore seems
to have crawled closer during the night,
proclaiming the coming of ice and snow.
You can stand in the now empty shallows,
in that indefinite boundary
between liquid and solid.
There are subcutaneous trails on the lake, veins
under pale white skin, passages for things seldom seen
in their secret migration, silent.
So you stay on the grimacing
shoreline and watch.

Winter

In the morning, they are out there:
tiny huts populating that inviolable space,
or what you once thought was inviolable.
No notice in the newspaper,
no message in the mailbox. Only a word on the wind,
on the wire that connects those who know, who belong,
who are part of this secret migration, silent.
(Not you.)

The woods offer refuge.
To walk, to feel solid ground underfoot,
under feet that fall heavily on old snow, creaking.
The dogs will leave you, abandon
shows in their noses and tails.
Something has just passed by, not creaking.
There are many tracks in the snow;
some you recognize, some you don't.
One set seems made by a mythic creature stopped
in its secret migration, silent,
to drink from the stream
where your dogs now lap.

Spring

Groaning, a ravenous monster
roaring, sits you upright
in bed in the middle of the night,
eyes wide open. The pained ice shifts
under the first warm pulse of spring.
In the morning you see that the huts
have gone, the trails have thickened, formed a pond.
Now only you are making tracks in the mud.

Summer

Anticipate the warm air, the sun-soaked
shoreline, water the golden color of ale.
Bathers lounge in those places,
both water and sand, purgatory
at any other time of the year.
The opposite shore has retreated.

Children will run through the forest,
brush past the furry evergreens
whose pointed embrace was so threatening
in the glowing darkness of winter.
Alienation comes in both seasons
and between them, you will leave your imprint
in the soggy earth for someone else
to see, who will wonder about
your secret and silent migration.

SUZI BANKS BAUM

Labels

Up the unfinished stairs, Maxie pounds to her attic bedroom in her fuzzy, gray felt boot liners. She carries every bit of wrapping paper she could rescue from the wild frenzy of Christmas morning. After that mayhem, Maxie has things to mull over, alone. She is still full from the Eggs Benedict Mom made this morning with thick slices of leftover ham. Christmas breakfast is Mom's special thing. She sets the breakfast table with Grandma Joan's pottery. Maxie thinks the bowls look like thimbles for giants. Grandma Joan makes each girl their own mug every Christmas, which adds to Mom's breakfast surprise. Late Christmas Eve, Mom sets the table after the girls are asleep, this year, with red placemats woven by Mrs. Anderson, and their new mugs. Mrs. Anderson is the school nurse at the elementary school where Maxie's mom teaches. When Maxie bikes past Mrs. Anderson's house, she sees her seated at a loom in the glassed-in front porch. The placemats were a housewarming gift for Maxie's family when they moved in last summer.

This morning, the girls bounced around so much they hardly noticed their new mugs. One year, the girls' mugs had tiny clay butterflies perched on the lips of each cup. This year, Maxie's was different from her little sisters' colorful mugs. Grandma scratched the clay of Maxie's mug with the names of the rocks they collect together. They are amateur rock hounds, Grandma and Maxie. They look for fossils and agates among the stones that litter the beaches of Lake Superior.

Maxie drops the shiny papers on the table she uses for a desk in her little attic room. She plops on to her unmade bed and feels the cozy closeness. Grandma Joan calls her bedroom a snuggery. She is the only person who visits Maxie up here. Mom's agreement with Maxie was that if she was going to sleep in that attic, she must keep it clean herself. So she does.

Maxie wraps herself in a quilt and studies the map of the Solar System she has tacked to the ceiling above her bed. The librarian gave her a whole stack of maps that come with a nature magazine Maxie reads at the library. The dark blue of the Universe calms her down a little. Her eyes trace each Planet's path, looping near, then far, far away from the sun. Winter in the Upper Peninsula feels like Pluto, so far from the sun, so cold.

She can hear the girls chattering to each other downstairs, playing with their new dolls, Weebles, they are called. Maxie didn't get toys this year, just books and socks, which she is happy about. But something else is on Maxie's mind, making her breakfast feel like a hard lump in her tummy.

Yesterday, on Christmas Eve day, they had to get to church early, since her younger sister, Marty, was one of the angels singing Silent Night in German for the Candlelight Service. Maxie's Confirmation Class was on cleanup duty for the Christmas Eve potluck, so she had to stay after. Mom took Marty and the littler girls home to bed right after the service. Mrs. Anderson, who helps with the Confirmation kids, agreed to drop Maxie off at home when they were done for the night.

Maxie's real purpose on Christmas Eve was Paul. The only boy in their Confirmation Class who was taller than Maxie, he is also the only one who doesn't tease her. Paul has brown eyes and a laugh with no hard edges. Maxie knows that Paul's parents are strict like her mom, so they will never be able to go to a dance together until junior year in high school. They sign up for Confirmation Class duty just to be together.

Last night, they were the dish drying team, Paul and Maxie. Paul put on a Santa hat after the church service and said, "Ho, Ho, Ho," every time one of the church ladies asked him to lift or carry something. Maxie dried every single coffee cup in the whole church. Heavy white mugs with a red stripe around the middle, she clanked them out of the rinse water, rubbed them dry with big linen towels, which she found by the hundreds, ironed and folded in the drawer marked "Drying Towels." The ladies of the church, the Dahlia Circle, make a big fuss about keeping the church kitchen organized. They use a label maker thing, which presses white letters in to skinny blue strips of plastic that are sticky on the back. All over the kitchen, the doors and drawers are labeled so you can find knives or the big red cans of Maxwell House coffee without first having to open every cupboard. Maxie wonders if she could borrow the label maker. It could help keep their winter stuff organized at home. They have about a hundred hats and mittens, which are always getting lost under someone else's coat hung on hooks in the back hall.

Every time Maxie handed Paul a dried mug she said something in French. She and Paul are in Monsieur Cote's Beginning French class and Maxie's accent needs a lot of practice.

"Bon jour."

"Merci."

"Je m'apple Maxie."

"Et toi, comme appelle tu?"

"Il est une cup ici."

Paul laughs and reaches the cups to the high shelf labeled "Christmas Coffee Cups." Maxie spies a beaded belt with words on it under Paul's sweater when he stretches up. She wondered where Paul went to get a beaded belt.

"Can I see your belt?" she asks with the next cups.

He blushes, and lifts his sweater up at his back. She can see, "Santa Fe" written in black beads.

"An early present from my crazy Uncle," he says.

"I've never been there. Have you?"

Paul frowns and shakes his head. They get back to work.

Mrs. Anderson packed up boxes with potluck leftovers for the shut-ins. Shut-ins are the old people who do not go outside in the cold on Christmas Eve. Her Confirmation Class did odd jobs for the shut-ins every season, raked their lawns or shoveled their walks, or helped move lawn furniture. Maxie couldn't figure out what made them shut-in, except that they didn't like to drive late at night, lift heavy stuff or be out in the cold.

Paul and Maxie helped Mrs. Anderson load the packed boxes into the back of her wood-paneled station wagon. Maxie wondered why a lady like her would have a car like that. She thought Mrs. Anderson's kids were all big and moved away. She'd have to ask Mom.

Maxie put on her navy pea coat and gloves. She kept her hat in her pocket so her hair would not get squished. Mom let Maxie iron her hair that afternoon. She had managed, with the help of pink hair tape, to give herself a Brady Bunch hairstyle.

Paul sat in the back seat and Maxie in the front so they could hop out whenever Mrs. Anderson stopped by the curb. Maxie would run up to the door to ring the bell. Paul followed up the steps with a box. They had to wait in the cold night air, chuffing clouds at each other, until the old timers would shuffle to the door to let them in.

"Mer-ry Ch-ristmas! Oh, you kids are so good to us. Come in out of that cold now."

Paul would slip off his boots and carry the box to the kitchen while Maxie stood on the rug by the door admiring the Christmas decorations and shouting over the carols turned up loud on their 8-track players. They always asked after Maxie's grandma, but not her grandpa because he died when Maxie was 4. She'd yell over "Hark the Herald Angels Sing," and give them the lowdown on Grandma Joan, how she was making bowls for an art gallery downstate. She wouldn't say anything about Grandma Joan marching in a protest against the mines or being arrested for chaining herself to an ancient tree up on the Yellow Dog Plains with a bunch of other activists last October. If she told them that, there would be a tirade about getting in the way of the logging companies or how her Grandma got in to "politics" after her husband died, like that was a very bad thing.

As soon as Paul would appear around the corner, always with two cookies in his hands, they'd hurry out.

"Mer-ry Ch-ristmas you kids. Tell Signe thank you, will ya' now? And watch yer step on that ice!" They'd holler out the door as Paul and Maxie slid down the icy sidewalk in their church shoes.

Back in the warm car, Mrs. Anderson sang carols in a soft whispery voice. It was late for all of them. Maxie loved the slow crunching sound of tires on the snowy streets. There were just a few cars driving carefully home from Christmas Eve parties, or the Midnight Mass at St. Anne's out by the highway.

Mrs. Anderson pulled up to Maxie's house. She could see Mom's light on in her room, but the rest of the house was dark. Their Christmas tree was in the front window, beaming tiny white lights out on to the snowy porch. It looked like stars had landed in their yard, where the lights touched the surface of the icy snow. Maxie hopped out. As she closed the car door, she heard Mrs. Anderson ask Paul to carry the last box up to her house. Maxie caught her breath. She got hot inside her coat. Her mom was not a shut-in. Paul bounced out to get the box. When he ran up alongside her, she tucked her chin under her jacket collar. He waited quietly while she struggled to get the storm door open and slid it wide enough for him to step inside with the box. Maxie took it from Paul. She said, "Merry Christmas" as quickly as she could. He answered, "Joyeux Noël," in a perfect accent, but she could not lift her eyes. He dipped out the door. She closed it with her backside. The kitchen wall was cool under her hot hand as she felt for the wall switch.

Since Dad left last spring, people had been dropping stuff off for them, even their Christmas tree. Somebody had left a note in the mail basket, with no name on it. The note said, "We have an extra tree. Come pick it up from the curb at 862 Ogden this afternoon." Maxie didn't understand why people thought her family needed help. Mom was a schoolteacher and they didn't buy new stuff, hardly ever, so they didn't need a bunch of money. But her mom always accepted the help, so Maxie unpacked the box. She lifted a large foil-wrapped still-warm lump, the ham. There was a Tupperware of Jell-O salad, another one with Ambrosia, a container of scalloped potatoes and a whole wrapper bag of dinner rolls. There was a carton of cream, which Mom would love in her coffee in the morning. Maxie hung up her coat in the back hall and shut the lights. She snuck up to the attic as quietly as possible.

Warm in the nest of her messy bed on Christmas afternoon, Maxie tries to make sense of things. She follows the lines of orbit of the Planets. She thinks about Paul's belt. She wonders if there are Lutherans in Santa Fe. Following the oval lines, Mercury, Venus, Earth, Mars, Jupiter, Saturn, Uranus, Neptune, Pluto–Earth looks like a small blue bead on a fancy necklace. Maxie studies each orbit and falls asleep.

Summer Sunset by Steven W. Huder

PAUL DOTY

Two for Harrison:

Old Men Lunch Bags

Reading Jim Harrison, simply because the narcissistic twenty something maple tree on the corner is drenched in a mongrel frost sticky tonguing. An autumn day lifting winter's little finger, so up with the prototype Northern Michigan hero: hard drinking man eye brow deep in a mid-life crisis convinced Keats' truth is just out of reach. Two days earlier at lunch a twenty something in yoga pants eating an asymmetrical cheeseburger dropping spare part pickles observed that those of us who brought lunch all had well-worn lunch bags. Three brown-beige bags worn to fallow corn husks, three middle aged ears of corn, three men eating unsustainable sandwich, chips, small portion of cookies in logoed cellophane bags. The most accomplished ear of corn quipped,

"My wife makes a hellova chicken salad," and acknowledging expertise acquired by time

segues to that accrued in the name of insulating middle age from the foibles of growing old.

Take for instance a large a collection of books by Jim Harrison bought mostly at used bookstores, which together affirm a resignation to appetite and the whiskey wrought journey to an interior resilience that saves you. Not a healthy sunrise view of traversing one's middle years, but it does expose the jangled nerves that open ears to the moods of young trees. Graceful aging is one part collecting books and paying attention to the well-made sandwich, and one part insisting you are not aging gracefully.

PAUL DOTY

Jim Harrison's Fate

Jim Harrison! Where are you? Fly fishing
on the River Styx bumming cigarettes from
Charon, or seated in Elysium on a huge pine
stump talking Northern Michigan similes
with Dionysus?

GERARD SARNAT

Lake Superior Sepia Seepage *Circa* 1952

When their names vanish like yesterday,
I pay a visit to the john.

Snapshots taped to the bathroom mirror:
Mac and my corduroy jacket

with that built-in belt unbuckled in front.
Kept there in case I forgot

next to Alexandra Lee picking us up
in her rugged nursery school van.

Mom demented, Daddio and the others gone
before Internet

once memories leak no trace, all evidence
is wiped off the face of this earth

except for those frayed photos.
Mac's short hair and baseball cap stand behind

helping me aim their rifle
while her partner, Lill, smiles approvingly.

Both were colleagues of Mommy's,
social work professors at the University of Chicago.

Pops asked, Since Mac 'n Lill can't have kids,
could they share us for the summer?

We'd drive through Watervliet, Michigan
where bearded Amishlike men from The House of David

played baseball in uniforms.
Lill taught me to fish for perch (I'd try to keep them alive

in an old trunk on the shore) in the oil-slicked
gas-smelling boathouse, how to row the dinghy.

Bunch of us'd motor to little islands to lunch
on meat-stuffed pasties — once or twice they let me steer.

Miss Lee (who wanted to be called Alex)
did not have children — I think.

Maybe the upbringing we soon rebelled from
wasn't exactly straight?

Superior Driftwood by Steven W. Huder

NANCY HIRSCHENBERGER

Why the Bull Elk Bugles

Once on a cold frosty evening on a long time ago, Misty, a sensitive loving elk maiden decided that there must be more to life than following her normal, unexciting routine. She was tired of pulling herself off the damp, spaghnum-moss bed in which she slept and quietly, before sunrise, tip-toeing through the leafy debris of the forest floor in order to search for her breakfast. The crunchy blades of green grass and tender new sprouts of pine seedlings for which she constantly hunted always tasted good but after a while, she longed for a munch of the once-tasted fall fruit which grew on the trees in the distant orchard. Also, her mother, Mother-Elk was spending more time teaching her new Fawn-Baby how to hide behind thick groves of cedar trees and clumps of cattails so that Fawn-Baby would be safe from stalking hunters and prowling wild cats. If that wasn't enough, Misty had this constant feeling that felt sort of like butterflies flitting around inside of herself, giving her a very uneasy feeling! She didn't understand what it meant, but she decided to venture out a little further than usual today and try to discover what glorious experiences might be out there waiting for her.

She moved stealthily over the next mossy hill and through the tree-lined ravine below. As she neared a shadowy maple stump in her path, a dark furry animal suddenly jumped out right next to her and she panicked. She dashed off to her left through the bushy swampland and didn't stop running until she could hardly breathe. She stood there shivering and panting, wondering what to do, but she gradually realized it was nothing but a harmless cotton-tail rabbit. As she quietly calmed herself down, she decided to wander over to the orchard which was now very near to her. There was a small, flowing stream to cross on the way and since she was very thirsty, for her throat was dry after her long run, she reached down to drink some of the refreshing cool water. Suddenly, she noticed, as she also heard, the reflected image of a remarkably handsome bull elk standing next to her ... Her heart started to beat furiously as she glanced up, shyly, at him, and as he gazed back he snorted a friendly hello. As they stood there, together, a special magnetic attraction, an attraction of the past, present, and future, wild in nature, combined their lonely spirits into one. Misty's thoughts of Mother-Elk and Fawn-Baby and all of the other familiar sights, sounds and friendships of her past life, just faded away as this new overwhelming feeling of love for her new companion, Bull-Elk took their place. Quite surprisingly to Misty, now free of those irritating flutters within her, she quietly walked off with Bull-Elk as he gently nudged her to follow him.

The next few weeks were full of the most enjoyable experiences that Misty had ever had. Sometimes they would play running and hiding games in the oak groves or in the bushy swamps. When they got hungry, they would carefully search for fat tender acorns under the oak trees, or wander near the flowing stream where the tasty green grass grew abundantly. Later on, when the nights got cooler and the smell of fruit was in the air, Bull-Elk would lead her to the orchard where they found and ate their fill of delicious, juicy apples. At night as the rippling brilliant orange-pink waves of the fading sunset swept over the land, they would find a mossy glen or dark cedar grove where they could settle down to sleep, nestling against each other for comfort and warmth.

One moonlit night as they lay huddled for warmth in their small glen, they were awakened by a sharp awareness of a change in the air! Their eyes began to smart and they were very thirsty. Misty sniffed the air as Bull-Elk, already on his feet, nudged her out in the dark, cold autumn air. In the distance they could see a brilliant orange glow in the sky, but it seemed strangely different than the big ball of fire that they saw, daily, on the same horizon. It was ominous and threatening and they could feel a sense of danger. By then, there were large puffs of curling smoky air forming weird shapes as they twisted and ascended skyward. Bull-Elk snorted to Misty and they headed, quickly towards the nearby water. When they reached the little flowing stream, other elk, as well as many other frightened forest animals, had already congregated and were heading in various directions away from the billowing, smoky fire. As the wind seemed to change its direction and swept the flames sideways, Bull-Elk and a friend, Stag-Elk decided to head up the tall, tree-lined hill past the stream, to try to find the safest path away from the danger area of the rapidly spreading fire. As the two brave elk passed over the peak of the tall hill, they heard a terrible whooshy, whistling sound as the fire, feeding on the dry timber of the trees below, swept through the treetops! It seemed to move like the flash of glowing light which pierced the forest during a summer storm! Quickly, the two elk hurried back to the area by the stream where Misty and the other animals had been waiting earlier. Bull-Elk's heart lurched and he ran fiercely in all directions as he searched the charred wasteland for his mate. Frantically, Bull-Elk and Stag-Elk bellowed out strange, mournful high-pitched cries as they looked for Misty. Because he felt such a loss, Bull-Elk would often start fights with other wandering male elk. Often during those long moon-laden fall nights after much heart-piercing trumpeting, they would charge, forcefully, into each other, breaking or ramming their proud horny racks until the contest ended in one fatal move for the weaker elk.

As the years went by, Bull-Elk never found Misty, but he never stopped searching for her. No one knows if Bull-Elk or Misty still live in the deep forest or if their spirits are still there, where they lived so happily, but one thing is certain. If, on a moonlit night in the autumn of the year, you are ever in the deeply-forested territory where elk like to live, you can still hear the bugling of the elk! Some say this piercing, unworldly, magnificent trumpeting is the spirit of Bull-Elk searching for his Misty.

Winning poetry and prose from The 16th Annual Young Writers Juried Exposition Petoskey, Michigan

The Crooked Tree Arts Center and Petoskey News-Review 16th Annual Young Writers Juried Exposition is supported in part by the Bob Schulze Fund for Creative Writing at the Petoskey-Harbor Springs Area Community Foundation, McLean & Eakin Booksellers and Walloon Writers Review.

CALISTA HOEKSEMA

The Demanding Pround

The demanding Pround
grows up from the ground,
and as soon as he sprouts
he whines and he pouts.
His temper is awful,
he's terribly rude,
and every day
he's in a bad mood.
He hurls insults all day
and lies all night.
He's nosy, he's grouchy,
and starts horrible fights.

I was tired of this
and knew what to do...

I chopped him all up
and made some Pround stew!

Ellsworth Public School Grade 5
First Place Poetry, Elementary School

CALISTA HOEKSEMA

The Rage of the Dragon

The mutated snail climbed a pineapple tree deep in the forest of the Angered Dragon. Suddenly a possessed monkey jumped up and hit him with an eyeball from his ear. The mutated snail fell to the earth and his shell cracked on the coral. The possessed monkey took the dead snail up to the fire cave and presented him as an offering to the Angered Dragon. The snail disappeared and a pile of tokens appeared in his place. The possessed monkey sighed with relief. The dragon accepted his offering of the week. The monkey gathered his tokens and flew home.

In the dragon's chambers, the dragon's captives bowed to the Angered Dragon as he prowled into the room. The captives included a mutated penguin, a possessed falcon, and a demon squirrel. These were just a few of the animals who had failed to make offerings each week. He was more violent to some. He blasted them off the face of the earth or he banished them to the desert of the possessed scorpion camels. Others who especially disgusted the dragon were brought to the chamber of the demon ax grinding wasp.

"The monkey barely made the time" the Angered Dragon bellowed. "The scorpion camels are hungry" he said and looked over to a quivering koala in the back of the cave. The koala was one out of a few animals who was not affected by the curse of the demons. The koala had not given his offering and was very afraid. "Take him away" the Angered Dragon said to the guardian flying lions. "NO!" the koala screamed. "Have mercy on me!" His pleas echoed through the cave and they heard the last scream ten times louder as he was banished to the desert.

"Anyone else?" the Angered Dragon said and yelled an evil yell as his stone heart beat wildly with anger. The whole mountain shook as the dragon laughed his horrid laugh. He went into his central chamber with a smile of pride and rage. The dragon had his robot slave get him some lava ready for bathing.

Down in the forest was a fight for life if you were a small animal. Many animals had been abandoned by their families. Possessed snails to mutated lizards were murdered left and right as the animals frantically tried to make offerings to the dragon before it was too late. Today was the last day and only one more hour of it.

If you were a monkey, you would have to worry about finding an offering and trying not to become one for a bigger animal.

But the next day would be Sunday, the Day of Redemption. An angel would come down and choose a faithful animal and cure him of his demon. The angel would also help to repopulate the forest to attain it back to its natural beauty. She would do this by planting more trees, flowers, and biobuds. The biobuds would grow into healthy forest creatures. But this Sunday was special. Every faithful animal would be healed. This special day would be called The All Time Healing.

All of the animals eagerly awaited this day. The dragon did too. He wanted regular servants just like every other great tyrant ruler. It was a wonderful day in the future. The next day at 11:30, all the possessed animals started to gather around to await the angel's presence. Even the Angered Dragon's servants came to be cured. At 12:00 all the animals covered their eyes as a blinding flash shone through all the forest.

A pale spirit floated down to the earth in the form of a red panda. "Greetings" she said to the circle of animals. "I grant you freedom from your possessors" she sang in her silky voice as she waved her magical paws. The animals each were brought up in a fluffy cloud as the transformation took place. After the renewal, the animals were brought back down. They looked and felt different. Shouts of joy were heard all throughout the circle. Nobody had a frown.

Meanwhile, the dragon waited for his servants to come back, but they never did. The demon that had tortured them had forced them to worship the dragon. The demon left, so they were free.

The dragon's rage grew twenty times and his eyes boiled a dark red. He exploded out of the cave soared over the forest, fire spewing out of his mouth. The angel saw this and flew over to where the dragon was. "This means WAR!" the Angered Dragon bellowed. "As you wish", the angel said calmly. It wasn't much of a battle because the angel just waved her shimmering paws and he was gone. He was banished onto the small moon Calbana. The only neighbors he would have were toxic gas whales.

The forest was in celebration. The jolly animals renamed their forest The Forest of Chances. Everyone could not stop cheering. It was wonderful, for now.....

Ellsworth Public School Grade 5
First Place Prose, Elementary School

JACK EARL

Baseball

I walk up to bat, the crowd is so loud,
my family is cheering, they sound so proud.
Their pitcher is good, he is a threat,
my bat is slippery, it must be the sweat.
The sun is big, it's in my eyes,
I want to win, I want the prize.
Then all of a sudden, the pitcher winds up,
I load my swing, I back up.
He swings his arms and lets it go,
he throws hard, on this pitch it will show.
It comes out of his hand, it looks like a curve,
my head is filling up with nerve.
I'm going to swing, my hands go back,
when all of a sudden, I heard a big crack!
Everyone waited, stopped in suspense,
I looked at it closely, it went over the fence!
Everyone screamed, we had just won,
because for the first time ever, I hit a home run!

St. Francis Xavier Grade 6
First Place Poetry, Middle School

GISELLE DAWSON

The Huntress and Her Prey

As the sun set, darkness spread across the woods like a spilled well of ink. Night settled and extinguished all faint wisps of light that remained. Time seemed to forget the dense forest; there were no crickets chirping, no owls hooting, no birds flying in the starless night sky. Nothing in the deadened woods moved. Everything was eerily silent and hushed, as if waiting for something to set it free.

Something had risen from its hiding. Its breath appeared to clear away the clouds in the sky; sending in a stream of clear moonlight and illuminating the dark. Its big brown eyes gleamed as it pawed the ground. Its antlers seemingly brushed the clouds with their tall golden majesty. It moved quickly, through the woods, but somehow, its hooves made no sound against the leaves.

But, just as fast, it was gone.

The knurled branches of towering trees twisted apart to reveal a path so overgrown and draped with shadows it was nearly impossible to see. Along it, a thin silhouette moved agilely through the tall oaks, quickly weaving in and out of the trees with flashes of silver. In her own mind, her pounding heart seemed louder than the roll of thunder; the whoosh of her breath seemed more powerful than a gale blowing the through the trees. But like her prey— she scarcely made a sound.

But, just as fast, she was gone.

There was a stream, winding through the forest, and its waters gently trickled over the mossy stones. The prey tipped its head to the cool water and let it flow into its mouth. It should have been peaceful, but instead it was eerily quiet, like nothing else lived or breathed. Something shattered the silence; the creak of a bow, the snap of the string, and the swish of an arrow piercing the air. But the prey was gone; the blade slicing merely a shadow and skidding off the watery stones with a splash.

The golden sun painted the sky pink, purple, and orange, blending together in streaks of color. The trees creaked as they stretched to awaken. The songbirds and the gentle breeze both sang over the waking treetops. Warm light blanketed the forest, and the stream sparkled as it rushed over the rocks in the riverbed, softly laughing as it fell on its way.

Then, the huntress and her prey were both gone, vanishing into the dawn's soft light.

Homeschool
Grade 6 First Place Prose, Middle School

MICHAEL WHENNEN

The Mad Writer's Manifesto: Inspired by 'The Mad Angler's Manifesto' by Michael Delp

I speak with the voice of writing
book, poem, paper, and pen,
for the rough drafts in sewn notebooks,
engraving morals, every place,
where the thoughts of mind gather
to remind me of the power of words.
I speak with the name of ink
with the gentle caress of motivation
even the ink which fortifies each stroke
every drop another transition from soul to paper.
I invoke the masses of words to take over the world,
to begin the thoughts and writing sure in the fact
that tomorrow another poem will rise, another story begin,
another writer will tire of their own words,
and seek inspiration within mine,
running up my paragraphs and diving into my worlds

I praise the writer's toolbox,
the metaphors, the careful
extensions laid throughout a piece,
the webs of interconnected words
coursing through bulky paragraphs.

I write in stanzas, multicolored stages,
my poem a living marker for how I crest pages,
multi-step fanboys, two-sided kennings and infinitive phrases.
When my eyes fall on blank pages I praise their potential,
my creativity shaping onto them words and worlds alike.

Writing is my heart searing across a white page
my soul aching to translate words, the secrets of gods,
into metaphors and three-dollar words on the cusp of an idea,
sifting themselves out in a dream.
I praise for the comfort of writing,
the feelings manifesting, converting that love and hatred to
words across a page. the sudden drive to write a poem
in the dead of night, words snatching me at the edge of sleep.
I embrace the hush of a pen dancing, the litany of holy singers:
Shakespeare, Poe, and Whitman.

I trust only the sweet smell of crisp paper
the scent of words festering with ideas,
the thoughts rising in my blood like an illness, a fever sent by
Erato to make her presence known, worlds jolting
through the veins to replace the words. the book that broke
the New York Time's bestseller list, the soul trader I most likely
have become.

Boyne Falls Public School Grade 12
First Place Poetry, High School

ELIZABETH DONOVAN

Dancing Under the Stars

Every stage of the day had its own magic. And I loved every one of them; the misty sunrise mornings; the golden tinted afternoons; the orange soaked sunset hours.

But the night was made for me. It was everything in my heart. Flying down the freeway with the windows rolled down. Smeared car headlights and reflections streaming in endless waves. Wind whipping at my hair, my hand stuck out the window dancing in the dark with a mind of its own. The radio pouring out lyrics perfect to scream along to: Come on world! Here I am! Bright stars pinned to the black sky, a snow globe full of diamond shards. The moon a comforting glow to light the spindly trees. Gas station neon lights blinking and sputtering like dying fireflies. Empty parking lots and abandoned parks - constant, unchangeable places unaffected by time.

My revelations always seemed to come at night, sweeping in like they had been waiting for the sun to set and me to lower my defenses. My revelations were usually unfamiliar, unwelcome thoughts during the daylight hours, but with the night came a different me: one more open and fearless. One night in particular I was feeling especially open and fearless; the stars were burning with a vengeance and the sky had cleared just for me. Despite my revelation's usual tendency to arrive when I was alone, I was not. My best friend was in my company.

We laid side by side on the cold pavement of my driveway, basking in the silver moonlight and talking aimlessly. The thing I think I loved the most about us was our absolute appreciation for each other's company. Whether we were interacting or simply sitting in the general vicinity of one another, we were content. There was something untouchable about finding complete comfort in another person who was not a member of your family. We found each other through what was surely random coincidence and yet we had decided that we loved each other unconditionally.

My face was tired from smiling (as it regularly was when we were together) and my eyelids were heavy. Our laughter petered out and we took in the night. The bugs were loud in their last hurrah before winter came to silence them. The air was frost bitten as it tugged at the sleeves of my sweatshirt, but my friend and I sat so close that our own individual heat warded the other's coldness away.

I sighed and spoke softly, "I wish every night could be like this." I could hear the wanting in my voice as clearly as I'm sure she could see it on my face. She tilted her head towards me and looked at me with eyes painted in washed out blue and silver watercolors. Her light hair resting on her gray sweater reminded me of a duckling's soft downy feathering.

"But then what would make tonight special?"

I waited a moment before responding, "What makes an ordinarily extraordinary night extra extraordinary?"

She shifted and laid her head on my shoulder, "Champagne. Velvet. Chocolates." Her eyes fluttered closed and she loosed a breath that rolled away like the smoke from a wizard's pipe.

My turn. "Music. Chandeliers. Extra cheesy pizza." She smiled with her nose scrunched up in a way that meant she loved us.

"And dancing," she added. I inhaled the night in all of its cold bewitching glory.

"Why don't we." It wasn't so much a question as it was a suggestion. She scrunched her nose up again and smiled.

"You're a dork." Which meant yes.

I hopped up and held my hand out towards her. Looking down at her I was struck with something like sadness. A sort of sadness that came from loving something so much that you thought your heart might just collapse in on itself like a dying star, beautiful in its destruction.

She slid her hand into mine and hauled herself up and onto her feet in a single fluid motion. As she moved closer I could hear the crickets chirping in rhythm with the wind's whistling and the creatures that only crept out at night all shuffling and picking their way through the leaves and trees. It was comforting to know that there were other living things out on an evening this magical.

Even the air had a sound: anticipation. Like it was holding its breath. She locked her fingers around my neck and I settled my hands on her waist. I smiled in a way that I knew was endearingly crooked; it had taken years to perfect this particular smile. She smiled in a way that was endearingly dreamy; it had taken years to perfect this particular smile.

We swayed harmoniously to the beat of our hearts. My nose was turning numb and her cheeks were rosy from the cold, but we stayed.

We stayed and we danced.

We couldn't be bothered with the cold because we were too busy finding our own music and its lyrics.

My revelation didn't come in a well-structured, gramitaculary accurate, nicely phrased sentence. It came as an ever expanding feeling. And even the word feeling can't quite describe it properly. It was like trying to cup slick opalescent oil in your hands even though you knew it would soon drip from your fingertips. The feeling was huge and fast. It was racing out of my mind as swiftly as it had entered. I desperately scrambled for the idea, trying to grab a fistful of it before it disappeared entirely.

The feeling that we were big and powerful and hungry. Queens of the vast and insurmountable world, and we were going to swallow it whole.

I tightly gripped that little handful of the feeling I had managed to seize, and I tucked it away.

Away into my heart where I could see it coiling around my soul. Keeping it safe and feeding it inspiration.

We danced under the stars and I felt infinite.

Petoskey Public School Grade 10
First Place Prose, High School

Contributors

BRETT ALLEN is a West Michigan author and U.S. Army veteran, originally from Fremont, but now residing in Ada, MI with his wife, two young children, and devious dog. When not writing and spending time with his family, he enjoys exploring the vast expanses of Michigan's bountiful breweries. For the past 20 years, Brett's made annual summer camping trips to the Pine River. "This story is my story from my first trip so many years ago," writes Brett.

MILTON J. BATES lives in Marquette, Michigan. He is the author of books about the poet Wallace Stevens, the Vietnam War, and the Bark River watershed in Wisconsin. Five Oaks Press published his poetry chapbook *Always on Fire* in 2016.

SUZI BANKS BAUM is a writer, artist, actress, teacher, community organizer, and mom. With roots in the Upper Peninsula of Michigan, she lives in the Berkshires of western Massachusetts. Suzi uses the written word, hand bound books, and photographs to say what she means. Her first book, *An Anthology of Babes*, celebrates the writing of women artists. Deeply curious about the thresholds we cross in to creative practice, she writes personal narrative with an ear for transformation though engagement with the ordinary. Suzi has an ongoing artist residency in Gyumri, Armenia, where she leads an art and writing workshop called New Illuminations. Published in *The Collection: Flash Fiction for Flash Memory* by Anchala Studios and *Writing Fire* by Green Fire Press. Find Suzi's work on *Easy Street, Literary Mama, Manifest Station, Asbarez, Rebelle Society, Mothers Always Write* and her blog, www.suzibanksbaum.com.

TOM CONLAN lives, writes, and tends his grape vines in the highlands of Northern Michigan. He has captained a Coast Guard Cutter, sailed the world's lakes and oceans, and now searches for the elusive brook trout in backwater streams. Tom's prose has appeared in print in *Vine Leaves Literary Journal, Issue #12, Tulip Tree Review*, in the anthology, *The Water Holds No Scars*, in *QU Literary Review*, and in *Walloon Writers Review*. Poetry in *The Avocet*, and *Outlaw Poetry*. His work was chosen as a finalist for the Annie Dillard Prize in the *Bellingham Review*. His lyrical memoir *My Jour-*

ney Begins Where the Road Ends... was released in June, 2017, from Mission Point Press. Tom attended the Iowa Writer's Workshop, holds a Master of Fine Arts in Creative Writing from Queens University of Charlotte, and a Master of Science from the US Naval Postgraduate School in Monterrey, California.

ANDREA DEJEAN writes: The poem was inspired by my many years spent on Black Lake, between Onaway and Cheboygan, and by one winter in particular during ice-fishing season while visiting my parents (who built a home on the lake in 1978 after having rented summer cabins there starting in 1961). And while my emotional attachment to Black Lake in particular and to the northern Michigan region in general remains strong, I am a permanent resident of France and have been for the past 25 years. I am the translator of a book on biodiversity and have published my own poetry and creative fiction and non-fiction in both independent and university-affiliated literary journals.

PAUL DOTY is a reference librarian at St. Lawrence University and resides in Canton, NY. A long time Jim Harrison reader, he has also published an essay on Jim Harrison's Sundog, "Life is Unbearably Vivid: An Essay on Sundog by Jim Harrison and Wuthering Heights by Emily Bronte" in the *Great Lakes Review*.

LINDA GALL is a lifelong resident of Gaylord and enjoys spending time with her family, boating, travel, and photography. She is the Charlevoix Photography Board President and loves wildlife, landscape and macro photography. She and her husband John have two married daughters and two grandchildren.

CJ GIROUX is a lifelong resident of Michigan. He teaches at Saginaw Valley State University where he serves as assistant director of its writing center and an editor of the community journal *Still Life*.

NANCY HIRSCHENBERGER grew up on a farm near Flushing, MI. She frequently traveled north to the family cabin near Atlanta, MI and experienced many adventures which shaped her love of Nature. One night in the Autumn, she experienced an amazing incident involving elk bugling. This influenced her writing. Nancy graduated from Central Michigan University with a Bachelor of Arts degree in Elementary Education. After teaching Fifth Grade in Shepherd, MI for two years, she moved to Crooked Lake near Petoskey, where she and her husband resided with their two daughters and son. She was a paraprofessional in the Petoskey Public Schools and obtained her master's Degree in Reading.

STEVEN W. HUDER is an amateur photographer with a passion for the woods and water of Northern Michigan. He lives in the Petoskey area.

J.W. JORDAN writes, "My family has been enjoying summertime in the Les Cheneaux Islands now for over one hundred years and counting. Growing up spending several weeks each summer at Cedar Haven, the family cottage on Marquette Island, has been a blessing and an irreplaceable part of my life. It is a place of rich family history and natural beauty that has become part of my being and identity. My wife Maren and I live near Indianapolis, Indiana. Our daughter, Madeleine, is enjoying life living in Brooklyn and working in Manhattan, New York. I thoroughly enjoy writing about past and current times on the island and I am honored to have been a prior contributor to the Walloon Writers Review. More short stories and a few photos can be perused on my blog, The Cedar Haven Reader (jottingsbyjon.wordpress.com).

KELLY TINGLE KAZMIERSKI is a multi-medium artist and creator of original and commissioned works of photography, pencil, pen and ink, acrylic, oil and mosaic. Kelly's most recent distinctions are highlighted with an Art Prize 2016 top-20 finalist selection, the publishing of her children's book The Girl with Spaghetti Hair, and a heritage photograph honored by the Harbor Springs Historical Society. Born and raised in Windsor, Ontario, former school teacher and veterinary technician, Kelly is a year-round resident of beautiful Harbor Springs, Michigan where her influences are rooted in the natural majesty of the Great Lakes and purity of animals and nature. Here, surrounded by inspiration, is where she works from her studio above the shores of Little Traverse Bay.

JESSE LINCOLN writes "Michigan has always been my home and I have always been enchanted by nature. I have a young son and the same seems to be true for him." Jesse currently lives in the Lansing area and love spending time with his young son.

CAROL OBERG began her writing career publishing poetry on greeting cards, world-wide, for Blue Mountain Arts., Inc. She was one of three featured poets in *Ancient Paths, issue 16,* where one of her ten works was nominated for a Pushcart Award. Carol has since published in *Bacopa Literary Review, Artifact Nouveau, The Fourth River, Madras Mag, El Portal, New Plains Review,* among others, with upcoming poetry in *The Chiron Review* and *Spillway.* She is semi-retired on a small inland lake in Michigan's Upper Peninsula.

CHARLES RAMMELKAMP grew up downstate in Albion, Michigan and his family has owned property on Old Mission Peninsula for 100 years. He presently lives in Baltimore, MD and comes to Michigan for two weeks every summer.

GREG RAPPLEYE'S poems have previously appeared in *Poetry, Shenandoah, The Southern Review, Virginia Quarterly Review,* and other literary journals. His second book of poems, *A Path Between Houses* (University of Wisconsin Press, 2000) won the Brittingham Prize in Poetry. His third book, *Figured Dark* (University of Arkansas Press, 2007) was first runner-up for the Dorset Prize and was published in the Miller Williams Poetry Series. His latest book, *Tropical Landscape with Ten Hummingbirds,* will be published in the fall of 2018 by Dos Madres Press. He teaches at Hope College in Holland, Michigan.

SHARON RUFF'S "The Impound Lot," was published in the 2017 issue of *Peregrine Journal,* and the poem, "For You I Write," was featured in the book, *Three Generations Fight Cancer Together,* published in 2017. She has been a guest writer for an on-line magazine and two websites as well as the Breathe Writer's Blog. Sharon holds a BS and MA in Business/Business Education and taught high school for several years followed by fifteen years of caring for her husband who lost his battle to MS. Since then, she has traveled to Ukraine and Africa speaking at women's conferences. "During this season of life, I am giving myself writing. I live in West Michigan near my children and grandchildren."

GERARD SARNAT won the Poetry in the Arts First Place Award plus the Dorfman Prize, has been nominated for Pushcarts and authored four collections: *HOMELESS CHRONICLES* (2010), *Disputes* (2012), *17s* (2014) and *Melting The Ice King* (2016) which included work published by Oberlin, Brown, Columbia, Johns Hopkins and in *Gargoyle, American Journal of Poetry* (Margie), *Main Street Rag, MiPOesias, New Delta Review, Brooklyn Review, Los Angeles Review of Books, Voices Israel, Tishman Review, Suisun Valley Review, Burningwood Review, Fiction Southeast, Junto, Tiferet* plus featured in *New Verse News, Eretz, Avocet, LEVELER, tNY, StepAway, Bywords, Floor Plan, Good-Man-Project, Anti-Hero-in-Chic, Poetry Circle, Fiction Southeast, Walt Whitman Tribute Anthology* and *Tipton Review*. "Amber Of Memory" was the single poem chosen for my 50th college reunion symposium on Bob Dylan. Mount Analogue selected Sarnat's sequence, "KADDISH FOR THE COUNTRY," for pamphlet distribution on Inauguration Day 2017 as part of the Washington DC and nationwide Women's Marches. For *Huffington Post*/other reviews, readings, publications, interviews; visit GerardSarnat.com. Harvard/Stanford educated, Gerry's worked in jails, built/staffed clinics for the marginalized, been a CEO and Stanford Med professor. Married for a half century, Gerry has three kids and four grandkids so far.

MELISSA SEITZ lives along the western shoreline of Higgins Lake, Michigan, with her husband. Her work has appeared in *The Bear River Review, The Dunes Review, The Lake, The Prose-Poem Project*, and various other journals. Read her blog for essays on life, music, and travel: https://lifeirruption.com/

PHILLIP STERLING'S most recent collection of poetry is *And Then Snow* (Main Street Rag, 2017). New poems have appeared recently in *The Georgia Review, Dunes Review, Split Rock Review, The MacGuffin*, and *The Lake*. He served as artist-in-residence for Sleeping Bear Dunes National Lakeshore in 2016

KATRINA VALUYEVA works in healthcare in parallel with a self-taught art practice with a focus on metalsmithing as well as occasional photography. She was born in Russia, grew up in Brooklyn, NY and found a permanent home in Indianapolis, Indiana.

ROBERT VIVIAN is the author of *The Tall Grass Trilogy, Water And Abandon* and two meditative essay collections, *Cold Snap As Yearning* and *The Least Cricket Of Evening*. His latest book, *Immortal Soft-Spoken*, was just published by Awst Press.

GLEN YOUNG paints houses on Mackinac Island and teaches school in Petoskey. He is a longtime freelance writer. His poetry appeared recently in *Thoreau at Mackinac,* and he served as editor of the collection *Beneath the Lilac Canopy.*

www.ingramcontent.com/pod-product-compliance
Lightning Source LLC
Chambersburg PA
CBHW060805210726
48292CB00013B/1852

* 9 7 8 1 9 4 3 9 9 5 9 0 5 *